The Birth
That We Call
Death

The Birth That We Call Death

Paul H. Dunn
Richard M. Eyre

BOOKCRAFT, INC.
Salt Lake City, Utah

Library of Congress Catalog Card Number: 76-5170
ISBN O-88494-297-X

First Printing, 1976

LITHOGRAPHED IN U.S.A. BY
PUBLISHERS PRESS
SALT LAKE CITY, UTAH

Acknowledgments

To the thousands everywhere who have need for reassurance and understanding.

To Marvin Wallin of Bookcraft for assistance in filling that need in the form of this book.

To Sharene Miner, in grateful appreciation for secretarial help.

To Richard Eyre, one of those rare and special individuals whose association has meant so much.

To my wife, Jeanne, whose insight, wisdom, and counsel give me the added depth, meaning, and strength.

Paul H. Dunn

For me, "writing" is the process of trying to capture in tangible words the thoughts that come in intangible spirit. Thus, for anything herein that rings true and provides real comfort, I credit the thought authorship of the Holy Ghost.

In my writing efforts I appreciate more than I can say the help of my wife, Linda, who has always been a better receptor than I of the intangible and a better judge than I of the tangible.

6 *Acknowledgments*

My confidence in the content of this book springs largely from writing and working with Elder Paul Dunn. His great knowledge of the gospel guides what we say and his great knowledge of people guides how we say it.

Richard M. Eyre

Contents

What we call "death" is the operation of life.
—Brigham Young

Death? Translated into the heavenly tongue, that word means life.
—Henry Ward Beecher

The only thing that really dies is death.
—Anon.

Chapter One
The Birth That We Call Death

I watched from the corner while people filed past the casket that held my close friend. Being here, standing in this place, didn't seem like reality —it was so hard to believe that he, a being I had known and loved, was gone from mortality, while I, a being known as Richard Eyre, remained. Even though his situation had worsened steadily for a month, and even though I had tried all during that month to help his family to see and accept the inevitable, now that it had happened my mind was numb and it was hard for me to accept the harsh reality.

From my corner I could see his family standing bravely by—his wife with a married daughter and two teen-age sons. I had tried to console and help that family ever since I knew he would die. Now I lowered my eyes and tried hard to recall, for my own comfort, the thoughts I'd given to them during the previous month.

During that last thirty days I had been in the Church library almost every evening after work, searching for comforting statements and phrases about death. I started my search by looking in the card catalog under "death"—but I ended up finding more of what I wanted under "life." I found that Christ and his apostles spoke of death under the heading of eternal life. The more I read, the more I learned to think of the transition we call birth in the terms Wordsworth used, as a sleep and a forgetting, and to think of the transition we call death as an awakening and a remembering. I gradually came to realize that (to one who knows of the preexistence and of this life's purpose and of the eternity that follows) death and life are not antonyms at all but almost synonyms, "fit-together" words that we use to describe two sides of the same coin. I found in my study that great thinkers of all ages, even though lacking in the specific knowledge of the restored gospel, had come to think of death not as an end but as a new beginning.

These were the thoughts that I had tried to bring to my friend's family—the concept of death as a *change* in life, not the *end* of life.

I stood now with bowed head, trying to recall the quotations and the ideas.

Seneca said:

The day which we fear as our last is but the birthday of eternity.

Rabindranath Tagore said:

Death is not extinguishing the light; it is putting out the lamp because the dawn has come.

Samuel T. Coleridge said:

Death but supplies the oil for the inextinguishable lamp of everlasting life.

Benjamin Franklin wrote to his niece upon the death of his brother (her stepfather):

> It is the will of God and nature that these mortal bodies be laid aside when the soul is to enter into real life. This is rather an embryo state—a preparation for living.
>
> A man is not completely born until he is dead.

Maurice Maeterlinck said:

> Let us accustom ourselves to regard death as a form of life which we do not yet understand.

President Brigham Young said:

> What we call death is the operation of life. . . . What we commonly call death does not destroy the body, it only causes a separation of spirit and body.

I had learned to think of death as birth—this life and this earth as the pre-natal beginning of the everlasting life that follows. Just as we each develop physical organs for this life during the pre-natal period in a mother's womb, so we develop spiritual capacities for the life to come during our "pre-natal" stay on this Mother Earth. These thoughts, interesting and appealing in the library, now became gripping and urgently true as I stood by, watching my friend's family and waiting for his funeral to begin.

I walked over closer to the casket now and realized that I couldn't imagine him as extinct, any more than I could imagine myself as extinct. I couldn't look at his face without knowing that it wasn't *his* face—just his body's face. I wasn't looking at him. I was looking at an empty shell, at the body which had been only the glove for the hand of his spirit.

I used that thought and tried again to ward off the heavy sorrow that pulled at me.

The line of people had dwindled now, and as I walked toward him his wife somehow sensed my need to regain some of the comfort I'd tried so hard to give her in the days before. She put her hand on my arm and said in a steady voice: "Don't try to fight the sorrow you feel. The only way to take sorrow out of death is to take love out of life."

How she could have known what I needed right at that moment (and how she summoned the strength to give it) I'll never know, but her words made me realize that I was fighting and resisting sorrow rather than accepting it and understanding it. Somehow, in her, sorrow was not bitter but sweet, a thing of beauty and deep meaning. She had never given up hope until the moment he died—and then, at that very instant, it seemed that her hope had transformed itself into the peace and assurance that I had been trying to discover for weeks. There was a calmness and a wisdom behind her soft tears that lifted her and refined her countenance. It made me remember a scripture I had found the month before but had not used in my attempts to comfort her. (I realized now that I hadn't used it because I hadn't understood it.)

> Thou shalt live together in love, insomuch that thou shalt weep for the loss of them that die. . . .
> —Doctrine and Covenants 42:45

Watching the sweet softness in her sorrow caused other quotations to come back to me—

words that I'd found in the library but failed to understand until now, as I saw them manifest in her.

Molinos said:

> Thou art never at any time nearer to God than when under tribulation, which he permits for the purification and beautifying of the soul.

An unidentified author said:

> Who never mourned hath never known·
> What treasures grief reveals,
> The sympathies that humanize,
> The tenderness that heals.

Another unidentified author wrote:

> For 'tis sorrow that works our pondering,
> and grief that teaches us to feel.

I was realizing now that my idea of comfort had been to *combat* the sorrow, to somehow *overcome* it with faith in God's wisdom and in the hereafter. It hadn't worked, not even on myself.

Now, in my friend's wife, I saw that real comfort was in the combination of sorrow and faith; that these two qualities were not mutually exclusive but compatible.

The way she bore the pain recalled to my mind the words of Henry Ward Beecher:

> There are many trials in life which do not seem to come from unwisdom or folly; they are silver arrows shot from the bow of God, and fixed inextricably in the quivering heart—they are meant to be borne—they were not meant, like snow or water, to melt as soon as they strike; but the moment an ill

can be patiently borne it is disarmed of its
poison, though not of its pain.

I could see and feel the presence of the Holy
Ghost in her, and I realized now that his presence
did not eradicate sorrow but, rather, mellowed it
and calmed it and made it sweet. The spirit I saw in
her (and that I now began to feel in me) was the
same "welling up," the same full, warm presence
that I had felt in testimony meetings and in
situations of great joy; a presence that always
brought tears to the eyes rather than drying them
away. I was suddenly aware that in the Sermon on
the Mount, Christ said, "Blessed are they that
mourn," and that it was to those who do mourn
that he promised comfort.

So I let the sorrow come, and I cried openly for
the parting from my friend as I filed from the
viewing room into the chapel for the beginning of
his funeral. As I accepted the sorrow it was quickly
accompanied and soon overshadowed by a deep
sense of gratitude for the life he had lived, for the
stewardship he had kept, and by the profound,
calm assurance of the Holy Ghost that I now felt.

For some reason, I remember very little about
the funeral service that followed. The one part I do
remember, however, is so vivid and clear that to
this day I can almost repeat it verbatim. It was a
story one of the speakers told about a sailing ship,
and I see it in my mind like this:

In a beautiful blue lagoon on a clear
day, a fine sailing-ship spreads its brilliant
white canvas in a fresh morning breeze and

sails out to the open sea. We watch her glide away magnificently through the deep blue and gradually see her grow smaller and smaller as she nears the horizon. Finally, where the sea and sky meet, she slips silently from sight; and someone near me says, "There, she is gone!"

Gone where? Gone from sight—that is all. She is still as large in mast and hull and sail, still just as able to bear her load. And we can be sure that, just as we say, "There, she is gone!" another says, "There, she comes!"

Rossiter W. Raymond said:

Life is eternal and love is immortal; and death is only a horizon, and a horizon is nothing save the limit of our sight.

Alexander Graham Bell said:

One door closes, another opens.

President John Taylor said:

While we are mourning the loss of our friend, others are rejoicing to meet him behind the veil.

As the funeral ended, I felt a love and closeness toward my friend's family and his other friends that was unlike any closeness I had previously experienced. I left with the conviction that in the sharing of sorrow, as in the sharing of any deep emotion, lies the basic organic relationship and unity of mankind. I also left with a greater understanding both of comfort and of the Comforter, and with new definitions—of *life* and *death* as synonyms; of *sorrow* as a word closely akin to *love*, and of "joy" and "sorrow" as compatible feelings.

It is on such occasions that one has his deepest feelings and his most profound thoughts. And while words fall hard and hollow upon a sorrowing heart, a person strives to find meaning in his feelings and attempts to make articulate his thoughts. Perhaps we should speak only of particular sorrow, for we can never judge another's grief, being able to know only our own.

Sympathy makes it possible for feelings to flow from one to another, giving us a glimpse of the wholeness of mankind. And within our own hearts we experience something of the suffering of others.

Sorrow, then, must be akin to love. In fact, what is sorrow but a tender side of love?

About a month after the funeral I visited my friend's family for the first time since his passing. It was at their initiative, not mine. They had invited me to dinner. I went, not knowing whether to expect continuing heavy sorrow or light, forced attempts to be cheerful. I found neither—instead, I found the spirit that J. R. Miller must have referred to when he said:

> The happiest, sweetest, tenderest homes are not those where there has been no sorrow, but those which have been overshadowed with grief, and where Christ's comfort was accepted. The very memory of the sorrow is a gentle benediction that broods over the household, like the silence

that comes after prayer. There is a blessing
sent from God in every burden of sorrow.

At the end of our meal, my friend's fifteen-
year-old son, the youngest, the one I had always
been closest to, asked if we could get together and
talk. I said yes, thinking that maybe now I could
help the boy in his readjustment and offer a truer
comfort than I had offered before. We set a time the
next day.

We met at the zoo because it was a fine, warm
spring weekday and the zoo's quiet paths and
benches were almost deserted. As we walked, I
bore to him the testimony I had of the eternal
nature of the soul and of the higher work I knew
his father was doing.

The longer I talked, the more I realized that he
already knew. He knew his father was alive in the
spirit world, and he knew that he would be with
him again. Suddenly, instead of trying to give him
answers, I wanted to ask him questions. I wanted
to ask about the changes I saw in him.

I had noticed them first the evening before, but
they were clearer now. He was still a fifteen-year-
old boy, but there was a strength in his stance and
a calm, clear light in his eye that was new. He
didn't look suddenly old or suddenly serious and
somber. Rather, he looked somehow more confident, more alive—and more peaceful and calm.

He was an unusual boy—I had known that for
some years—but I didn't realize how unusual until
the end of that walk in the zoo, until he had
finished answering my questions.

He said that somehow his father's death had

made him understand things—things that gave him insight into other people and confidence in himself. He had discovered that the reason why people are afraid of death is that they are afraid of the unknown. Fear made most people absolutely unwilling to think of death; but his father's passing and the prayers that followed it had shaken him out of that fear. Now he did not fear death and did not fear thinking about death.

After that kind of beginning by a fifteen-year-old boy, it is easy to understand why I found little more to say. I simply nodded my head and continued listening to what I have since come to regard as a profound set of observations.

He said that he saw three great advantages in thinking about death:

1. Thinking about it prompts questions and brings about the thought and effort necessary to acquire an understanding of it. We do not fear what we understand.

   (Now I could see why he looked more confident.)

2. Thinking about it and about its inevitability and unpredictability makes us more aware of life, more tuned in and more appreciative of each moment and aspect of life.

   (Now I understood why he looked more alive.)

3. Thinking about it and about the eternity that follows makes the worries and trials of this short earth-life seem smaller and easier to bear; thus it becomes easier to live with the problems and difficulties of daily life.

(Now I understood why he looked more peaceful and calm.)

I asked where he had gained the insights and he told me that he thought they were prompted by the Holy Ghost and perhaps by the spirit of his own departed father.

I wouldn't have had anything more to say, except that I remembered a Shakespeare quotation which I told him he had just helped me to understand.

> Be still prepared for death—and death or life
> Shall thereby be the sweeter.

The spirits of the just. . .are not far from us, and know and understand our thoughts, feelings, and motions, and are often pained therewith.

—Joseph Smith

The spirit has not changed one single particle of itself by leaving the body.

—Heber C. Kimball

Chapter Two
Where Is He Now?

When a loved one has passed on, two kinds of comfort are available. One lies in the condolence and love of friends, the soothing words of poet and philosopher, and the comforting presence of the Holy Spirit.

The other lies in knowledge and insight—knowledge of where the loved one is and insight into what he is doing.

Through revelation to his appointed prophets, our Heavenly Father has given us this knowledge. Because of his love for us and his understanding of our need for comfort, he has told us with positive clarity and strong assurance where our loved ones go.

By studying his revealed word, we can be sure of six things:

1. That the spirits of all men, immediately upon death, go to the spirit world to await the resurrection.

2. That, for the righteous, the spirit world is a place of joy and peace.

3. That it is also a place of continued progress and a place of missionary work, where

those who have received the gospel can teach it to those who have not.

4. That our departed loved ones are changed only in that they are temporarily separated from their bodies; that in personality, character, and characteristics they remain the same; that the spirit does not change.

5. That the spirit world is not far removed from earth but close by, though invisible to our mortal eyes.

6. That some departed spirits know and understand our thoughts and feelings; that they are aware of us and retain their love for us.

The following statements of prophets give us this knowledge and assurance. Note how positive and precise they are, how specific and complete they are. Indeed, it has been said that through the restored gospel we know more about the state and condition and activity of our loved ones after they die than we knew about them during short earthly separations.

Behold, it has been made known unto me by an angel, that the spirits of all men, as soon as they are departed from this mortal body, yea, the spirits of all men, whether they be good or evil, are taken home to that God who gave them life.

And then shall it come to pass, that the spirits of those who are righteous are received into a state of happiness, which is called paradise, a state of rest, a state of peace, where they shall rest from all their troubles and from all care, and sorrow.

—Alma 40:11-12

When the spirits leave their bodies they are in the presence of our father and God; they are prepared then to see, hear and understand spiritual things. But where is the spirit world? It is incorporated within this celestial system. Can you see it with your natural eyes? No. Can you see spirits in this room? No. Suppose the Lord should touch your eyes that you might see, could you then see the spirits? Yes, as plainly as you now see bodies, as did the servant of Elijah. If the Lord would permit it, and it was his will that it should be done, you could see the spirits that have departed from this world, as plainly as you now see bodies with your natural eyes.

—Brigham Young

The spirits of the just are exalted to a greater and more glorious work; hence they are blessed in their departure to the world of spirits. Enveloped in flaming fire, they are not far from us, and know and understand our thoughts, feelings, and motions, and are often pained therewith.

—Joseph Smith

When a person who has always been good and faithful to his God lays down his body in the dust, his spirit will remain the same in the spirit world. It is not the body that has control over the spirit, as to its disposition, but it is the spirit that controls the body. When the spirit leaves the body, the body becomes lifeless. The spirit has not changed one single particle of itself by leaving the body.

—Heber C. Kimball

For death is no more than a turning of us over from time to eternity.

—William Penn

Birth, in the same terms, turns us over from eternity into time.

—Present authors

Chapter 3
From Eternity into Time into Eternity

Imagine for a moment that you are about to cross the country on a train. You get on board, and as the train starts you find yourself sitting next to a fine person who is making the same journey that you are. Since the trip usually takes almost four days, you begin a serious attempt to get to know each other. You find that you have much in common, and by the time the train steams into the darkness at the end of the first day you feel a remarkable closeness and begin to feel that the relationship you are forming may be the most important part of your journey.

After a sound night's sleep in the Pullman car, you rejoin your friend and the two of you spend another day relating to each other and experiencing the journey together. Your rapport grows still stronger, and you find yourself feeling a little sorry that the day passes so fast. By the second night your train is deep into the flat middle plains, and as you fall asleep you are thinking about the things you want to find out and talk about with your friend the next day.

In the morning you return to your seat and find, to your dismay, that your friend is gone. When you inquire, someone tells you that he got off during the night.

Got off during the night? But he had a destination very near your own, and you had planned on having the next two days with him, and there was so much more left to say! Suddenly you realize that you never did find out quite where he came from or just who he really was, and that you never did learn why he was on the train or exactly where he was going. Worst of all, you realize that you don't know whether you'll see him again—that you don't know how to find him or contact him.

The feeling is a mixture of sadness and frustration which together produce something in between bitterness and anger. Why did he have to leave? Did someone or something make him leave? Should you be upset at him for leaving or at someone else who made him go against his will? It's not so much that he's gone, it's that you don't know *where* he's gone and you want so much to see him again.

At that point the porter comes down the row to your seat. The message he leaves is very simple, but it changes night into day and bitterness into joy. He tells you that your friend was indeed going to the same place as you—that he was going there to see his father. During the night the train received an emergency message which instructed your friend to get off the train at the next stop and catch a plane to get home more quickly, because his father needed him right then. The porter leaves you a phone number so that you can contact your friend as soon as you arrive.

The simple message of the porter turns your frustration into peace. You are still sorry to miss the two days of discussion you had anticipated with your friend, but your sorrow is no longer bitter or blind; rather, it is sweet with the knowledge of where he is and the assurance that you will see him again.

The sorrow we taste with the loss of a loved one can be bitter or sweet, depending on one ingredient—the ingredient of knowledge; the simple, pure knowledge of our origin, our purpose, and our destination. The restored gospel gives us this knowledge. It tells us our origin; it reveals our purposes on earth; and it teaches us of the life hereafter, assuring us that loved ones will meet us there and that death is a temporary separation and not an utter loss.

As in the imaginary journey on the train, the sense of temporary separation that comes to one who knows the plan of salvation does not carry the sting and panic of permanent loss.

Benjamin Franklin once said:

> Our friend and we were invited abroad. . . . His chair was ready first, and he is gone before us. We could not all conveniently start together; and why should you and I be grieved at this, since we are soon to follow, and know where to find him.

Any dear possession, if separated from us for good purpose, and if returned in even better condition, produces joy rather than agony and peace rather than frustration.

One man loses his billfold containing a large sum of money. Another, with the same amount, sets goals and makes a planned investment. Both are now separated from their money, but one feels the bite and bitterness of permanent loss, while the other anticipates the day when he will retrieve his investment and enjoys the knowledge that it will probably grow in the meantime.

A loss we cannot comprehend or accept (and a loss that is considered permanent) is bleak and stark and comfortless; but a temporary separation as a part of a goal and plan is acceptable and, in a way, even joyful. The loss of a loved one—the parting of the spirit from the body—is not a permanent loss, neither is it a separation we cannot accept or comprehend. Rather, it is indeed an indispensable part of the goal and plan of God.

The goal and plan of God—in their comprehension lies true and lasting comfort and the ability to view death as Jacob did: " . . .Death hath passed upon all men, to fulfill the merciful plan of that great Creator. . . ." (2 Nephi 9:6.)

God is the literal father of our spirits, and Christ, the Firstborn, is our eldest spirit brother. We stood with them in the preexistence and may have heard our Father state his goal: "For behold, this is my work and my glory, to bring to pass the immortality and eternal life of man." (Moses 1:39.)

God had achieved immortality and eternal life

in a perfected, resurrected body. His goal was that we should become like him. As an infinitely wise father he had achieved ultimate joy, and as an infinitely good father he wanted us to become like him and thus to share that joy.

In that preexistence there were three broad differences between ourselves and our spirit Father, differences that had to be overcome if his plan was to be fulfilled and we were to become like him. First, God had a body, a glorified, perfected physical body that gave him certain capacities that we did not have. Second, he had power and intelligence and knowledge far beyond ours. Third, he was perfect and had mastered great character-istics that we had not.

We realized, as he did, that we could begin to overcome these differences only through the experience of a mortal existence on a physical earth. This realization, and the prospect of gaining physical bodies and experiencing earth life, aroused within us such gratitude and elation that we and all the hosts of heaven "shouted for joy." (Job 38:7.) There in the preexistence we must have had certain insights that we lack now, insights into the great value of earth experience and into the importance of that experience in God's plan of eternal progress.

We anticipated the joy of being able to relate to both spiritual and material things. We knew we needed bodies to feel with, to learn with, to react with.

In October conference in 1899, President Joseph F. Smith spoke of the joy he felt, a joy perhaps not unlike what we felt in the preexistence anticipating mortality: "I rejoice that I am born to live, to die, and to live again. I thank God for this intelligence. It gives me joy and peace that the world cannot give, neither can the world take it away."

Having defined both his goal (that we should become like him) and the vehicle for that goal (a physical earth), God ordained a plan, a plan that would bring about his goal, a plan for the salvation of his children.

Another plan was presented—by Lucifer, a son of the morning. It must have had the appealing, safe sound of a guarantee, for Lucifer's promise was, "I will redeem all mankind, that one soul shall not be lost. . . ." Apparently he would do this through coercion, making sure we all did what was necessary for salvation. Hence his plan contained no opportunity for failure. And all he asked for himself was everything—the full credit, the whole glory.

While Lucifer's plan and its author were rejected, the Father's plan was wholeheartedly accepted by Jehovah (Jesus Christ), the Firstborn. It called for agency and initiative. It included free choice and the opportunity for both success and failure. Because of its freedom, it contemplated pleasure but also pain, virtue but also vice.

Because it was realistic, it anticipated sin and error which, unatoned for, would permanently separate men from God. Thus Jehovah offered to be that atonement, to come to earth himself, to gain a body and, as Jesus Christ the Only Begotten Son of the Father, to willingly sacrifice his life for the redemption of the world.

As spirits we realized that through the operation of this great plan of salvation Adam would fall, bringing spiritual death and mortality upon mankind. Jesus Christ would atone for Adam's transgression so that, just as all men would die, all would subsequently be made alive (1 Corinthians 15:22), and thus physical death and physical resurrection would become two automatic transitions in eternity. Christ's atonement would also be the propitiation (1 John 2:2) or payment for everyone's sins so that, as we would repent, those sins could be removed, thus allowing us to overcome spiritual death as well as physical death. (Alma 42:7-10.)

There is as much comfort in the knowledge of a "forever backward" as there is in a "forever forward." Knowing where a loved one came from, why he was here, and that he achieved the basic purpose of his earth life, turns death from "the terrible unknown" to "a necessary step in the attainment of an immortal body and in the achievement of our eternal goal."

If, in the preexistence, we looked forward to birth, which was the leaving of our Father and our eternal family, how much more we must have looked forward to death, which would be a later and essential step in the coming home!

Mortality is the prerequisite to immortality; it is by passing the tests and gaining the progress of this world that men obtain eternal life. Thus death (passing from time into eternity) is as important and as wonderful as birth (passing from eternity into time), and both are among the essential transitions in the Father's plan for our salvation.

If there had been no council in heaven, there would have been no physical creation; if no physical creation, no Fall; if no Fall, no birth into mortality; if no mortality, no death; if no death, no resurrection; if no resurrection, no exaltation or eternal life. Thus death takes its place as one indispensable step in the great and good plan of our Father. To take away death, as Alma states, would frustrate the whole plan of redemption. (Alma 12:26.)

In our preexistent life we must have been somehow wiser, with eyes more open, since we chose the plan of free choice—the plan void of guarantees. We recognized the need for opposites and for testing—and we knew that many of us would fail. We realized that Lucifer's plan did not meet the goal of the Father, which was that we should return to him as beings like Him. We knew, with Christ, that we could become like the Father only if we proved ourselves through faith, only if we learned by experience and by overcoming adversity, only if we perfected ourselves by choosing good over evil, right over wrong, light over dark, progression over retrogression.

Two-thirds of the hosts of heaven, ourselves among them, apparently were able to see that the Father's plan was designed to meet the desired objectives. The plan provided a physical body which, through Christ's atonement and our ultimate resurrection, *would* become immortal and *could* become perfected. Yet it also provided a mortal probation for that body, in which we could grow and perfect ourselves by being subject to pain and difficulty and death. We must have understood that without darkness one can never know light, and we must have realized that, through the mortality the plan embodied, we could learn true joy through our contact with sorrow.

Thus no man comes into this realm of earth without suffering. As Augustine said, "God had one son on Earth without sin but never one without suffering." The Bible itself bears this out, telling us that even Christ, the implementer of the plan, is subject to the principles of that plan: "Though he were a Son, yet learned he obedience by the things which he suffered." (Hebrews 5:8.)

Suffering and sorrow and death, then, are necessary and constructive parts of mortality. Through the centuries, this great truth has been understood by many and phrased beautifully by a few:

Elder James E. Talmage said:

No pang that is suffered by man or woman upon the earth will be without its compensating effect . . . if it be met with patience.

An unidentified author wrote:

Pain stayed so long, I said to him today,
"I will not have you with me any more,"
I stamped my foot and said, "Be on your way,"
And paused there, startled at the look he wore.
"I, who have been your friend," he said to me;
"I, who have been your teacher—all you know
Of understanding love, of sympathy
And patience I have taught you. Shall I go?"

President Brigham Young said:

What can you know, except by its opposite?

Who could number the days, if there were
no nights to divide the day from the night?
Angels could not enjoy the blessings of
light eternal, were there no darkness. All
that are exalted and all that will be exalted
will be exalted upon this principle. If I do
not taste the pangs of death in my mortal
body, I shall never know the enjoyment of
eternal life. If I do not know pain, I cannot
enjoy ease. If I am not acquainted with the
dark, the gloomy, the sorrowful, I cannot
enjoy the light, the joyous, the felicitous
that are ordained for man. No person,
either in heaven or upon earth, can enjoy
and understand these things upon any
other principle.

In the midst of Joseph Smith's incredible trials
and sorrows, the Lord spoke to him in Liberty jail:
"All these things shall give thee experience, and
shall be for thy good." (Doctrine and Covenants
122:7.)

Elder Orson F. Whitney said:

It is through sorrow and suffering, toil and
tribulation, that we gain the education that
we come here to acquire and which will
make us more like our Father and Mother
in heaven.

Henry Ward Beecher said:

It is trial that proves one thing weak and
another strong. . . . A cobweb is as good as
the mightiest cable when there is no strain
upon it.

John Newton said:

Trials are medicines which our gracious
and wise physician prescribed because we

need them; and he proportions the frequency and weight of them to what the case requires. Let us trust in his skill and thank him for his prescription.

Edwin Markham said:

Only the soul that knows the mighty grief can know the mighty rapture. Sorrows come to stretch out spaces in the heart for joy.

Thomas Fuller may have said it in the fewest words:

No cross, no crown.

The grief of death may be the fuel, our understanding of God's plan the oxygen, and the love of God the heat that makes the refiner's fire burn. It clears and refines, consuming the dross and leaving the imperishable part intact and stronger than before.

Indeed, many have used the refiner's fire as an analogy for this earth's experience.

Jonathan Edwards said:

The surest way to know our gold is to look upon it and examine it in God's furnace, where he tries it that *we* may see what it is.

E. H. Chapin said:

The brightest crowns that are worn in heaven have been tried, and smelted, and polished, and glorified through the furnaces of tribulation.

Henry Ward Beecher said:

We are always in the forge, or on the anvil; by trials God is shaping us for higher things.

We often want to say: "Yes, yes, I know, I know, but this pain or this sorrow is *too* great. I cannot grow from it because it is more than I can bear." Perhaps we are standing or sitting when we say this, rather than kneeling and asking God for the strength we lack.

Sometimes it helps to remember what President Wilford Woodruff said:

> We have been called to pass through trials many times, and I do not think we should complain, because if we had no trials we should hardly feel at home in the other world in the company of the prophets and apostles who were sawn asunder, crucified, etc., for the word of God and testimony of Jesus Christ.

Physical death preceded by physical birth and succeeded by physical resurrection—these are the three inevitable transitions of eternity. Tertullian said, "It is a poor thing to fear that which is inevitable." Cicero added, "No man can be ignorant that he must die, nor be sure that he may not that very day."

Inevitable yes—but always there is the question, "Why now?" Why did God take the young mother from her small children, the little boy from his parents, the retired husband from the wife when all they had left was each other?

Why, indeed? The question, "Why now?" is a difficult one to answer, but thank goodness it is not we but God who answers it. Aren't we glad that God didn't leave the details up to us? As Elder

Richard L. Evans has asked, "When *would* we be willing to lose those we love?"

Since we cannot see backward beyond the veil or forward beyond the grave, we cannot fully answer the question, "Why now?" We are like the child who sits watching the TV repairman replace a small complex part and asks, "Why?" We cannot always understand the reasons or the timing, but we *can* develop the faith to know that God knows—and the trust that in his eternal plan all things can work for our good. Indeed, if you, with your limited perspective, were to choose the time of death, you might have kept Abinadi or Joseph Smith from a martyr's reward. You might have saved Christ from death and prevented the Atonement. You might never allow your own father or mother to go to their reward. You might have healed Paul or Job and robbed them of the strength they were to gain. Thus it is not ours to ask, "Why now?" but to accept by faith the wisdom and eternal timing of God, the eternal timing Elizabeth Barrett Browning may have sensed when she said, "On the earth the broken arc; in heaven, a perfect round."

Another "why" question, just as often asked and perhaps more easily answered, is, "Why a righteous man?" or, "Why an innocent child?" or, "Why this person who had been blessed by the holy priesthood that he would live?" Why does death so often take the innocent, the good, the blessed, and spare the wicked and the unworthy? The answers lie back in the preexistence, back when the two alternative plans were presented. Remember that it was Lucifer's plan that would have forced everyone to be righteous. It was the Father's plan (and ours) that called for agency, for opposites, for physical lives subject to circumstantial adversity and weakness and even to accidental death.

When we chose to accept that great plan, we knew that there were laws governing free agency, laws of natural consequence that God would not tamper with or break. We knew that the free will of men's minds would sometimes lead to improper uses of agency that would affect their lives and the lives of others in harmful ways. We accepted the risks and consequences and trials of free agency and mortality because we knew it was the path leading to a likeness with God.

If we could understand our agency now as well as we did then, we would be less inclined ever to view death as a punishment. Furthermore, we would realize that death is not always a "calling home," that it is often simply the natural consequence of the plan of agency which we once chose to follow and are now exercising.

Again, faith is called for to believe in the wisdom of this great and good plan, faith to accept God's will over ours and to trust his judgment over our desires. A great test comes when sincere prayers and priesthood blessings for the life of a dear one are answered negatively.

Of course, priesthood blessings often *do* heal the sick and they are always (if properly performed and understood) a great and positive comfort.

When a person is called home after a faithful priesthood blessing, we have the comfort and assurance that it was his appointed time to go and that God has called him home. As President Spencer W. Kimball has said:

> We are assured by the Lord that the sick will be healed if the ordinance is performed, if there is sufficient faith, and if the ill one is not appointed unto death.

Speaking of our "appointed time," President Kimball went on to say, "We can shorten our lives, but I think we cannot lengthen them very much."

Thus, when one leaves us in spite of our faithful prayers and blessings, we can be comforted in knowing that it was his time, and we can be lifted by the scripture, "If they die they shall die unto me." (Doctrine and Covenants 42:44.)

Indeed, one great purpose of life is that of a test, and one great test is our ability to accept what we do not fully understand—to say, "Thy will be done," and then to ask for the Comforter to give us peace and assurance even in those matters we cannot yet comprehend.

Satan's plan would have made earth life into a programmed, predestined routine with as little chance for real growth or progress as for failure, a distant, limited kind of earth without real experience or true comprehension.

There is a story of a great university scientist who wanted to explore and understand a great volcano. He was presented with two possible methods. One involved little risk but was limited in its potential result. It consisted of instrument

readings and thermal tests and of observation of
the volcano by looking down into it from the top of
its cone. The other method contained considerably
more risk but potentially great results. It involved
being lowered down into the volcano at the proper
time and actually seeing and experiencing the
various elements that the scientist sought to learn.

By analogy we might say that when we faced a
similar alternative, we chose the latter course. We
were lowered into mortality and we will be lifted
out of it through the atonement of Jesus Christ and
the resurrection. While we are here, we control our
own destiny according to our willingness to
experience and grow and learn. The professor in
the volcano was aware of certain safety rules and
scientific laws, the observation of which would
determine his condition when he would be lifted
from below. Similarly, we know of commandments
and principles which will govern our condition
when we are lifted up by the resurrection.

In all his words, Christ seemed to teach us that
our concern should not be for the body but for the
spirit, our grief not for physical death, where spirit
and body separate temporarily, but for spiritual
death, where man and God separate permanently.
Heber J. Grant gave this insight in the April
General Conference in 1945 when he said:

> And may we always remember, because it
> is both true and comforting, that the death
> of a faithful man is nothing in comparison
> to the loss of the inspiration of the good
> spirit.

Philosophers from all ages have sensed the fact that mere physical death is not man's great enemy. Socrates said:

> Be of good cheer about death and know this as a truth—that no evil can happen to a good man, either in life or after death.

It is interesting to expand the comparison between physical and spiritual death. In a physical sense, all men will have eternal life because all men are born twice and die only once. We are all born physically, we all die physically, and we will all be resurrected physically.

There are also three very similar spiritual transitions, but only the first two are predetermined. We were born spiritually to God the Father, and we became separated from him by the veil when we came into mortality. The third spiritual transition, however, unlike the resurrection, is up to us, and it is a choice between life and death. We will either die a spiritual death by allowing our unrighteousness to separate us forever from God, or we will be "born again" of the Spirit through faith, repentance, baptism, the Holy Ghost, and continuing righteousness.

And so it is, as with your friend on the train. Knowledge of where our loved ones came from, why they were here with us, where they have gone in death, and where we can join them—this knowledge cannot remove the sorrow from death, nor should it, but it can turn bitter grief into sweet sorrow and can give us comfort and teach us peace.

Our birth is but a sleep and a forgetting.
                              —William Wordsworth

Our death is an awakening and a remembering.
                              —Present authors

Is death the last sleep? No—it is the last and final awakening.
                              —Sir Walter Scott

We sometimes congratulate ourselves at the moment of waking from a troubled dream...it may be so at the moment of death.
                              —Nathaniel Hawthorne

Chapter Four
An Awakening and a Remembering

A woman told of the experience she had when her father died. He had been ill and in pain for some time, and many called his passing a blessing. The thing the woman remembered most, even though some years had passed, was the peace and serenity that seemed to come over her father in the brief moments immediately preceding his death. She said it was as though the pain had suddenly been traded for a relaxed, soft tranquility that permeated every fiber of his being. The lines of stress and pain slid from his face and were replaced by a peaceful smile. She said that the moment of death was beautiful and pleasant and serene, not only because it marked the end of his suffering but also because the actual physical process of death seemed to be so pleasant.

Others have supported her conclusions about the pleasantness of the moment of death. Dr. Félix Martí-Ibáñez said that the actual moment of death

> is suffused with serenity, even a certain well-being and spiritual exaltation, caused by the anesthetic action of carbon dioxide on the central nervous system.

Dr. William Hunter, an eighteenth-century physician, uttered these words in the final moments of his life:

> If I had the strength enough to hold a pen, I would write how easy and pleasant it is to die.

Derby spoke of his friend's response to death, which was almost identical to that of Dr. Hunter:

> Cullen, in his last moments, whispers, "I wish I had the power of writing or speaking, for then I would describe to you how pleasant a thing it is to die."

Thus it would seem that, regardless of whatever pain and suffering may precede death, death itself, the actual transition from time into eternity, is in the physical sense a peaceful and pleasant experience.

However pleasant the moment of death is physically, it is spiritually one of the most exciting and joyful moments of eternity. Like opening from the inside the door of a darkened room, one who dies emerges into the light of the spirit world where there will be friends and family waiting to greet him. Elder Charles A. Callis gave his testimony of this when he said:

> I have been with elders who died in the mission field, and a moment or two before they departed this life their faces have been overspread with a gleam of recognition of beings not of this world; they have uttered the names of loved ones long since gone

and then have peacefully gone to their eternal rest.

President Brigham Young said:

> There is no period known to them [the dead] in which they experience so much joy as when they pass through the portals of death, and enter upon the glorious change of the spirit world.

On this earth we view death from the perspective of one who stays behind, much as a man views a long journey when he is sending someone else off rather than going himself. He puts his friend on the train or plane and waves goodby, only able to imagine what the trip is like and what the friend will find when he gets where he is going.

If we could glimpse, for even a moment, the glory and excitement that a departed one faces when his eyes close on time and open on eternity—if only we could glimpse this, perhaps there would be more understanding in our sorrow and more joy in our grief.

We know almost enough, through scripture and revelation, to imagine what death's awakening may be like. Lift yourself for a moment from your own shoes and into the role of one who is departing from this earth. You close your eyes for the last time on the sights of this world and become aware that you are being pulled and lifted up and out and away from your body. You feel somehow lighter, perhaps both in weight and in illumination. Your eyes, this time spiritual eyes, now become open, and you are aware that you see and hear and feel and sense things which were closed to you while on earth.

Because you somehow have senses you lacked before, you can see the realm of spirits which you now enter. You recognize some of those you see. There is great rejoicing as they reach out and you embrace in the light of love and peace. You already miss your body, and somehow you now understand its importance, but you know it will be returned to you in the resurrection; and so you go forth meeting and remembering those you knew before.

President Joseph F. Smith said:

> ...Those from whom we have to part here, we will meet again and see as they are. We will meet the same identical being that we associated with here in the flesh.... Deformity will be removed; defects will be eliminated, and men and women shall attain to the perfection of their spirits, to the perfection that God designed in the beginning.

Jean Paul Richter said:

> Each departed friend is a magnet that attracts us to the next world.

President Brigham Young said:

> We cling to our Mother Earth and dislike to have any of her children leave us.... But could we have knowledge and see into eternity, if we were perfectly free from weakness, blindness and lethargy with which we are clothed in the flesh, we should have no disposition to weep or mourn.... It is true it is grievous to part

with our friends. We are creatures of passion, of sympathy, of love. . . . Should we not. . . rejoice at the departure of those whose lives have been devoted to doing good. . .?

Thus we know that the spirits of all men, as soon as death occurs, go directly to the spirit world where they await the resurrection, the final redemption and the judgment. As Alma says, "There must needs be a space betwixt the time of death and the time of the resurrection." (Alma 40:6.)

In general terms the spirit world, to which all spirits go at death, is divided into the abode of the righteous (paradise) and that of the wicked. (Alma 40:11-14.) After his death, the Savior bridged the gulf between them by bringing the gospel to the spirits in prison. (1 Peter 3:18-21; Moses 7:39.) Since that time, righteous spirits have been called to minister and teach the gospel to those who did not have it on this earth. Thus the spirit world is a place where those who had no opportunity to hear and accept the gospel on earth will have that opportunity, so that they can "be judged according to men in the flesh, but live according to God in the spirit." (1 Peter 4:6.)

It has been said that all truly deep and meaningful happiness stems from one of two sources: (1) service, helping and giving to others; and (2) anticipation, looking forward to and waiting for something important or fine. If indeed these are the two key sources of joy, the spirit world must offer great potential happiness, because it contains the greatest conceivable opportunity for service and holds in its future the event most worthy of eternal anticipation. A righteous spirit in paradise can teach other spirits the most important and indispensable knowledge in the universe and anticipate the greatest event: the glorious resurrection which makes possible the continuing eternal progression of the righteous.

Speaking of the great service and mission being performed by the righteous in the spirit world, President Brigham Young said:

> Compare those inhabitants on the earth who have heard the gospel in our day, with the millions who have never heard it, or had the keys of salvation presented to them, and you will conclude at once as I do, that there is a mighty work to perform in the spirit world.

If you can imagine the happy anticipation of a boy who has been away at a severe and demanding boarding school and who now returns to the beautiful home of his father whom he loves dearly—if you can imagine that happiness and then magnify it a million times, then perhaps you can glimpse the joy of a righteous spirit awaiting his glorious resurrection.

The joy we anticipate in the spirit world will come into full fruition in the resurrection, when our spirits will reunite with perfected resurrected bodies, our own bodies which we will rejoice in finding again and which will be immortal and incorruptible such that we will never again lose them.

One of the best attested facts in sacred

scripture is the resurrection of the Lord Jesus Christ, and one of the Savior's own most repeated teachings is his assurance that we too will rise from the grave. No two facts are more clearly and explicitly stated in sacred scripture than these—the reality of Christ's resurrection and the certainty of ours. The apostles witnessed the wounds in Christ's resurrected body and watched him eat the fish and the honeycomb. They went forth testifying, as he had, that, just as all men would die because of Adam, so also all men would live because of Christ.

President David O. McKay said:

> If Christ lived after death, so shall men, each one taking the place in the next world for which he is best fitted. Since love is as eternal as life, the message of the resurrection is the most comforting, the most glorifying ever given to man; for when death takes a loved one from us, we can look with assurance into the open grave and say "He is not here," and "He will rise again."

In the resurrection the spirit will re-enter its body, which initially will be in exactly the same state as when the spirit left it. Bodies that were sick, infirm or deformed will then be restored to health and perfection, apparently almost instantly —as Amulek says, to a "proper and perfect frame." (Alma 11:43.) Nor will age at time of death determine a resurrected being's appearance. President Joseph Fielding Smith said:

> Old people will not look old when they come forth from the grave. Scars will be

removed. No one will be bent or wrinkled.
. . . Of course, children who die do not
grow in the grave. They will come forth
with their bodies as they were laid down,
and then they will grow to the full stature
of manhood or womanhood after the resurrection, but *all* will have their bodies fully
restored.

Thus we know that those who lose little
children and are worthy will not only be reunited
with them but will have the blessing and opportunity of raising them in the glorious circumstances of the resurrection. Joseph Smith gave total
assurance regarding the place of small children
who die:

The Lord takes many away, even in
infancy, that they may escape the envy of
man, and the sorrows and evils of this
present world; they were too pure, too
lovely, to live on earth; therefore, if rightly
considered, instead of mourning we have
reason to rejoice as they are delivered from
evil, and we shall soon have them again.

Byron must have sensed this same truth when
he said:

Heaven gives its favorites—early death.

It is in the resurrection that our joy can become
full. Many have tried to imagine the beauty and joy
that will be felt in the resurrection. Among them
was President Lorenzo Snow, who said:

Nothing is so beautiful as a person in a
resurrected and glorified condition. There
is nothing more lovely than to be in this
condition and have our wives and children
and friends with us.

We know that marriages and family ties can endure beyond the grave. The Lord assured Joseph Smith of this and revealed the sacred temple ordinance of temple marriage "for time and all eternity." Studies and opinion polls have shown that most people who profess belief in a hereafter believe also that relationships and friendships and love will continue beyond the grave. Though the official theologies of other churches do not accept eternal marriage, individuals everywhere do. Andrew Jackson epitomized this hope and belief when he said, "Heaven for me will not be heaven unless I find my wife there."

In addition to the joy of family relationships extended forever into the eternities, just try to imagine the excitement and potential of having an eternity before you. Think of the kind of goals you might have if you had thousands of years to plan them and forever to carry them out.

In his supreme wisdom and in his sublime love, God has laid out before us a plan of such excitement and such beauty that it is difficult, while in the flesh, to fully comprehend it. As we learn it, though (by outward study of the word and inward study of our souls), we are lifted to higher realms, we face more easily the trials of our lives, and we feel the joy that can go with the sorrow of bereavement.

The Lord said to the Prophet Joseph Smith, "Wherefore, fear not even unto death; for in this world your joy is not full, but in me your joy is full." (Doctrine and Covenants 101:36.)

Life is real! Life is earnest!
And the grave is not its goal;
Dust thou art, to dust returnest,
Was not spoken of the soul.

—Henry Wadsworth Longfellow

Chapter Five
The Assurance Beyond

It was Job who posed the question of the ages: "If a man die, shall he live again?" (Job 14:14.)

It was Christ who answered it: "Because I live, ye shall live also." (John 14:19.)

Indeed, it is harder not to believe in the immortality of the soul than to believe in it. We are creatures of logic, and God's logic is infinite. We mingle our logic with our faith and thus receive the assurance beyond.

William Jennings Bryan spoke beautifully of the *logic*:

> If the Father designs to touch with divine power the cold and pulseless heart of the burned acorn and make it to burst forth from its prison walls, will he leave neglected in the earth the soul of man, who was made in the image of his Creator?

Ralph Waldo Emerson spoke of the *faith*:

> All I have seen teaches me to trust the Creator for all I have not seen.

President David O. McKay and Elder Charles

Evans each spoke of the logic with still greater insight. From President McKay came this:

> I believe with all my soul in the persistence of personality after death. I cannot believe otherwise. Even reason and observation demonstrate that to me.

And Charles Evans said:

> Some...believe that all human knowledge dies with the mortal tenement, that faculties, trained by years of laborious study, in other words, that the soul, the grandest work in the universe, of infinitely more value than worlds, ends at death's touch, and is annihilated.

> Imagine...every faculty of the soul falling into utter disuse, all the treasures of the mind instantly lost—this most intricate and wonderfully constructed apparatus cast away forever.

> What an awful thought.... Methinks no greater creative failure could be planned. It would be the very climax of irrationality—ignorance supreme.

Many men combined their logic and their faith (both of which taught them of the soul's immortality) and came to see the beauty that is in death.

Walt Whitman said:

> Nothing can happen more beautiful than death.

Charles Frohman said:

> Death is the most beautiful adventure in life.

George Eliot said:

> Those only can thoroughly feel the meaning of death who know what is perfect love.

Charles Kingsley said:

> And so make life, and death, and that vast forever one grand sweet song.

Indeed, it is impossible that anything so natural, so necessary, and so universal as death should have ever been designed by God as an evil to mankind. It is, instead, a necessary transition in eternity. Only in an eternal frame of reference can death be properly viewed and understood. President Spencer W. Kimball has expressed that thought in these words:

> If we look at mortality as a complete existence, then pain, sorrow, failure, and short life could be a calamity. But if we look upon the whole life as an eternal thing stretching far into the pre-mortal past and into the eternal post-death future, then all happenings may be in proper perspective and may fall into proper place.

In this eternal perspective death can be not only understood but appreciated. Benjamin Franklin seemed to have this appreciation when he wrote his own epitaph:

> The body of Benjamin Franklin (like the cover of an old book, its contents torn out, and stript of its lettering and gilding) lies here, food for worms. Yet the work itself shall not be lost, for it will (as he believed) appear once more, in a new and more beautiful edition, corrected and amended by the Author.

The authors had lunch with two men who worked together for the same company. One was close to retirement, the other was expecting to be promoted to the retiring man's position. It was interesting to us to observe the differences inherent in viewing one's retirement and one's promotion. The man awaiting promotion was excited, anxious, filled with anticipation. The one approaching retirement was sometimes sullen and sometimes seemed almost scared.

From this it might be concluded that we all want progress more than we want the end of progress.

Death is a promotion rather than a retirement. The concept of heaven as a place of harp-players resting on fluffy clouds is insignificant and unappealing when compared to the true kingdom of heaven where man will progress and develop and grow eternally, with this earth life as an important and useful foundation but without the frailties and weaknesses that often impede our progress here.

Many great thinkers, even without the illumination of the restored gospel, have been able to see the hereafter as a place of great progress. Victor Hugo said:

> The nearer I approach the end, the clearer I hear around me the immortal symphonies of the worlds which invite me. It is marvelous yet simple. For half a century I have been writing my thoughts in prose, verse, history, drama, romance, tradition, satire, ode and song—I have tried all; but I feel that I have not said a thousandth part

of that which is in me. When I go down to the grave I can say like many others, "I have finished my day's work," but I cannot say "I have finished my life's work"; my day's work will begin the next morning. The tomb is not a blind alley. It is an open thoroughfare. It closes in the twilight to open in the dawn. My work is only beginning; my work is hardly above its foundation. I would gladly see it mounting forever. The thirst for the infinite proves infinity.

Hugo's view of eternal progress led him to write a poem:

> Be like a bird
> That pausing in her flight
> A while on boughs to light,
> Feels them give way
> Beneath her and yet sings,
> Knowing that she hath wings.

In our eternal flight we have paused briefly on the boughs of earth, and it is our testimony of Christ's gospel and the Spirit of the Comforter that become our wings and make life and death one grand sweet song.

Postscript
The Formula for Eternal Life

The departing of a loved one is a part of our mortal test. If the separation is understood, if faith is applied, if the Comforter is sought and found—under these circumstances sorrow can be sweet and we can learn and grow from the experience as God would wish us to.

In one manner of thinking, it is not the departed but the bereaved that we should be concerned about at the time of death. The departed one is in the spirit world and in the care of his Father; but we who remain behind are left to decide for ourselves whether the separation will teach us strength and faith or bitterness and despair. It is we who remain that need guidance, who must still work out our own salvation within and amidst the trials and experiences of mortality.

There is a pattern for mortality that will always yield the desired result of eternal life if it is followed properly. We might almost call it a formula, so constant is its effect; though admittedly it does not conform in all respects to the conventional usage of the term. This "formula" becomes particularly important and applicable at the time of separation from a loved one through death:

Truth + Obedience ÷ Opposition
−Discouragement and Bitterness × Patience and Time = Eternal Life and Exaltation

(Truth plus obedience, divided by opposition, minus discouragement and bitterness, multiplied by patience and time, equals eternal life and exaltation.)

The formula works every time, just as surely as two plus two always equals four. Equally certain, however, is the fact that if one of the equation's elements is omitted the end result will not be reached.

Let us view the elements of the formula one at a time.

Truth: Within the gospel of Jesus Christ we *have* the truth. We know of the immortality of the soul and of the universal reality of the resurrection. We know of the eternal nature of God's family and of our own temple-sealed families.

Obedience: We believe that through the atonement of Christ, all mankind may be saved, by obedience to the laws and ordinances of the gospel. All blessings will be obtained by obedience to the laws on which they are predicated. Obedience is the first law of the order of heaven, the first law of the kingdom. Obedience to a law is the price we pay to become master of that law.

We know that an obedient, righteous person will dwell in joy and peace in the spirit world as he awaits the resurrection. We know that those who need repentance and greater obedience will have a chance to achieve both in the spirit world.

Opposition: The passing of a loved one is one of the clearest and most universally experienced forms of this life's opposition.

We know opposition is necessary. We know it can lead to greater compassion, greater faith, a greater measure of inner strength. We know that this earth's opposition is a test that we must meet in order to become more like God and more worthy of his presence. Opposition tries to weaken and divide; but if it is endured with faith and prayer it strengthens us, refines us, and leads us closer to eternal life.

Discouragement and Bitterness: These are tools of the adversary. If we yield to them, if we let them into our hearts, they will push aside our hope and faith; they will allow opposition to conquer us rather than strengthen us.

We know that part of life's test is to overcome discouragement and bitterness. We know the importance of sometimes forcing a smile and holding our head erect even as the tears roll down our cheeks. We know that Christ endured the ultimate pain and sorrow without ever exhibiting bitterness and discouragement, and we know that our eternal goal is to be like him.

Patience and Time: If we can meet the formula up to this point, and if we can do it all with patience and sweetness of purpose, time and its passage becomes a great blessing and a healer of all wounds.

We know that God's plan cannot be thwarted. We know that good must triumph over evil in the end. We know that the rewards of the kingdom of heaven will be so magnificent and the joy so great that our earthly trials will seem small and insignificant by comparison.

Eternal Life and Exaltation: God, the Father of us all, has said, "This is my work and my glory, to bring to pass the immortality and eternal life of man."

We know that he will meet his goal. We know that the sorrow caused by a loved one's passing is a part of his plan. We know that he stands ready to give us the strength we need to endure—if we have the faith necessary to ask and the courage necessary to follow his formula for eternal life.